You knit me together
in my mother's womb.

June 30, 2019

Congratulations, Brad and Kasey! If you're
not already amazed by the love you have
for baby Luke, you will be soon! and
just think — God's love for you is greater
still! We will be praying for you as
you parent this precious child.

With love,
Noah, Kristen + Evelyn
Sheppard

Visit Melissa Panter, the author and illustrator, at www.melissapanter.com.

Summary, "An alphabet book featuring an animal mama nursing her baby for each letter of the alphabet."

First Softcover Edition

Mammal Mama

An animal alphabet book that supports breastfeeding.

written and illustrated by
Melissa Panter

A IS FOR ARMADILLO

B IS FOR BAT

C IS FOR CARIBOU

D IS FOR DOLPHIN

E IS FOR ELEPHANT

F IS FOR FOX

G IS FOR GIRAFFE

H IS FOR HIPPO

I IS FOR IMPALA

J IS FOR JAGUAR

K IS FOR KANGAROO

L IS FOR LION

M IS FOR MANATEE

N IS FOR NARWHAL

O IS FOR ORCA

P IS FOR POLAR BEAR

Q IS FOR QUOKKA

R IS FOR RACCOON

S IS FOR SEAL

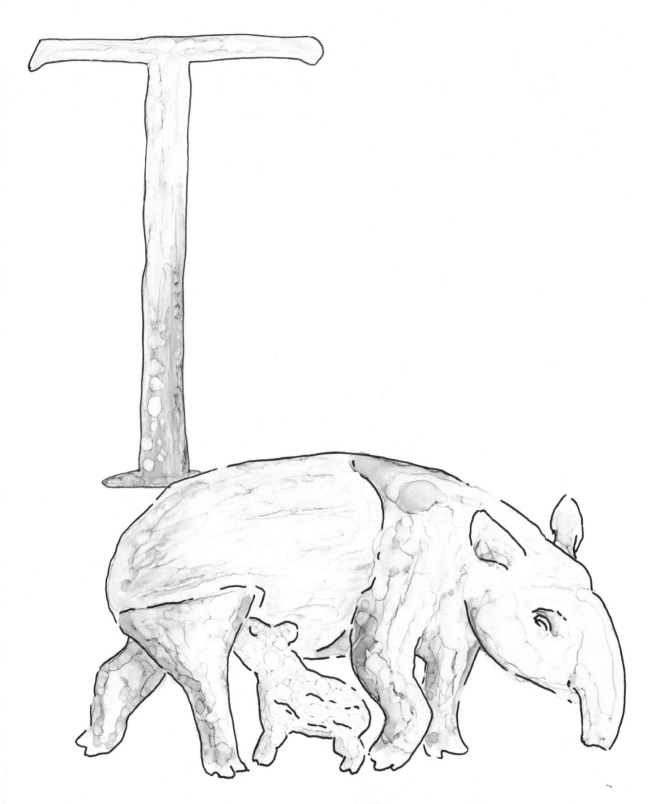

T IS FOR TAPIR

U IS FOR UNICORN

V IS FOR VICUÑA

W IS FOR WARTHOG

X IS FOR XOLO

Y IS FOR YAK

Z IS FOR ZEBRA